For Karen...

(in folklore) An ugly creature depicted as either a giant or a dwarf.

Someone who leaves an intentionally annoying or offensive message on the internet, in order to upset someone or to get attention or cause trouble.

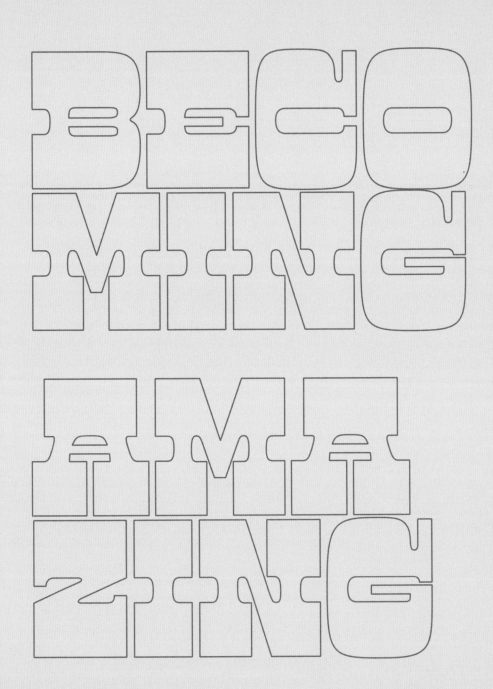

BECOMING AMAZING

Before we begin, I'd like to address the sceptics out there. I can hear some of you saying "you ain't no hero, you're a troll and a menace to society." But before you judge me, allow me to tell the story of how I got here.

In 2018 I went through a tough period in my life. It was more than tough, it was a full on mental breakdown. I won't go into the details of why I ended up in such a state (that's a whole new book in itself) but looking back, as painful as this experience was, it was the best thing that ever happened to me. After all, it's brought me here talking to you guys. Now some of you reading this may be going through a tough time right now, and I urge those of you to keep reading. I promise to have you laughing by the end of this book and, who knows, you might adopt a new outlook on life, one that will lead to a happier you.

My depression and anxiety had totally put a pause on my life. I was on meds and hadn't worked for seven months. I was at rock bottom. But the great thing about rock bottom is that you have nowhere else to go other than up and that rock is a great foundation to build a new you. Besides being desperately miserable, all I knew was that I had to do something to change my situation. The meds didn't really work for me; they may have taken the pain away, but I was left feeling numb from top to toe. So I decided to scrap them and find another way to feel like the old me again. I did some soul searching and asked myself the simplest of questions. What makes me happy?

I thought back to the last time I genuinely felt some sort of happiness and purpose. Of course, my family and being a dad were the first things that sprung to mind, they were the only things that had kept me going. But I was looking for something other than that.

Then it hit me... making people laugh had always been my passion. From being the class clown as a kid to writing satirical posts on social media which would often go viral, seeing people react to something I had done or said with a smile or a laugh was infectious.

Over the years I had toyed around on social media with my comedy. I would write sardonic comments laying into the endless posts I was seeing at the time warning of ridiculous scams that were simply untrue. To poke fun at this, I started posting my own warnings of scams based on the silly things we would do as children. It transformed me...

WARNING!!!

Wes Metcalfe

Warning!!!! Please share, dont become a victim of this scam. Today I was walking through Sheffield city centre when I was approached by a smartly dressed man who asked me if I would like to smell his cheese. As he asked this he gestured his hand towards my nose which was in the extended palm position. Being a lover of cheese I saw no harm in taking the man up on his kind offer.

As he brought his hand to my nose what I hadn't noticed was that his other hand was in the clenched fist position at the base of his extended palm. When his finger tips reached my nostrils I could neither see or smell the cheese and it was too late to retract as his now perfectly aligned fist of the other hand was travelling towards my nose at speed, which struck me with considerable force. There was never any cheese! This was a scam to catch me off guard and punch me in the nose. No matter how much you love cheese do not accept offers to 'smell my cheese' off people you don't know.

Please share and stay safe!

Sam Skinner

All i can say is you dumb shit

Amanda Savage

This was the thing in the eighties 😁 gave and received many a bloody nose.

Alan Tait

Holy shit these comments are funnier than the post, I'm sure there are some people here that actually think this happened in real life.

Do you people think that soap operas are live action?

MY CHRISTMAS COMPLAINT TO SKY

Then there were the times I'd make my own complaints online (yes, I know... I used to be a complainer too). But I wasn't someone to take matters as seriously as others often do. Instead I would complain somewhat tongue-in-cheek which generally prompted a great reaction from the companies dealing with me.

Wes Metcalfe > SkyHelpTeam

Wes Metcalfe
Last Christmas I signed up to Sky Q, but the very next day my Q Box wouldn't play. This year to save me from tears, I'm going with @virginmedia

Sky Help Team
Last Christmas we gave you Sky Q, but the very next day you had some tech issues. This year to save you from tears, We're going to assist you further ☺

Wes Metcalfe
Once bitten and twice shy,
I've kept my distance but still your programmes catch my eye.
Tell me baby what offers you have for me.
Well it's been a year so how do you intend to keep me.
Merry Christmas I wrapped it up and sent it.
With a note saying unsubscribe me, I meant it.

MY CHRISTMAS COMPLAINT TO SKY (CONTINUED...)

Wes Metcalfe

Now I know what a fool I've been, but if you make the right offer you will fool me again.

Both Sky and Virgin were quick to join in with the Christmas banter...

Sky Help Team

We don't want a lot for Christmas.
There is just one thing we need.
We don't care about the presents.
Underneath the Christmas tree.
We just want you for our own.
More than you could ever know.
Make our wish come true.
All we wanted for Christmas is you, Wes!

Virgin Media

If this is the case Wes, I have a little song for you also;
Well I wish it could be Christmas every day
When the V6 starts singing and the recordings begins to play
Oh I wish it could be Christmas every day
So let the bells ring out for Virgin Media

And then there was the time I found a dead worm trapped within the cellophane on a cucumber I had bought from Tesco. I instantly took to Tesco's Facebook page demanding justice for this poor worm who I'd named William.

After a few fairly standard responses from Tesco, my complaint was eventually answered by an employee called Rob who shared a similar sense of humour. With each exchange there would be poems and re-written songs in memory of William the Worm. I even shared pictures of the funeral I held in my back garden. Still, to this day, there stands a memorial bench outside the Tesco in Dinnington in Sheffield where the cucumber was purchased. The internet seemed to love this exchange between company and customer. The post soon went viral with news publications from all over the world reporting the story…

Read all about it. The story of William the Worm hit the headlines in 2016.

BBC NEWS

Tesco customer finds a worm in his cucumber and his complaint goes viral

Daily **Mail**   MORE STORIES

Tesco customer holds a 'funeral' for the dead worm he found on his cucumber - and the store responds with a beautifully written tribute

≡ **OK!**

CELEBRITY NEWS   TV   VIP CLUB   ROYAL   LIFESTYLE

LIFESTYLE

You will never believe what happened when this customer found a WORM on his cucumber

A compassionate shopper's interaction with the insect takes an odd turn

The dead worm was found trapped underneath the cellophane wrapping and a funeral was held in my back garden.

A TRIBUTE TO WILLIAM THE WORM

Tesco responds with a rewritten version of Oasis' Wonderwall – Wonderworm.

TESCO > Wes Metcalfe

Tesco

Well Wes,

What a beautiful tribute to such a beautiful worm; I think we're all comfortable in the knowledge that he'd be wanting us to celebrate his life today, and I've spent my free time listening to classic hits such as Boom Boom Pow, Pump It, Meet Me Halfway and Where is The Love in his memory; I'm sure he'll be looking down on us with much appreciation.

To continue the day of celebration, and to really incorporate a musical themed tribute, I've adapted a classic song in his honour from the back of your excellently constructed poetry piece.

I'm sure you have a live band there today who will be oh too familiar with this track... Are you able to get them to cover this for me?

Here goes...

Today is gonna be the day that we're gonna celebrate for Will,
He's gone, and now we're feeling sad, we know it's a void we cannot fill,
I don't believe that anybody, feels the way we do, about you Will...

Back beat, the word is on the street that you'd travelled many many miles,
I thought we'd seen it all before, but you've gave us memories and smiles,
I don't believe that anybody feels the way we do, about you now...

And all the grass you'd wriggled through is inspiring,
And all the time that Wes spent trying to revive you...
There are many things that we, would like to say to you
But we cannot now...

Because maybe,
You're gonna be the worm that saves me,
I think we've learned,
You're our wonder worm!

Hope this helps, thanks for keeping us in the loop today Wes; I'm currently raising a cup of tea in William's honour.
Enjoy the celebrations through the night.
Sincere Condolences
Rob- Customer Care

Wes Metcalfe

Rob that would have meant so much to William ... I'm pretty sure he was into the whole Brit pop scene – he had that dark greasy grungy look about him.
Once again you and your team at Tesco have moved us all with a brilliant Oasis Tribute.....
Allow me to join in and respond with a reworded classic from the same era...

Blur – Wormlife
Wiggling is a preference for the habitual mud dwellers known as...
WORM LIFE
Avoiding the morning feed as a preference to bird seed is known as...
WORM LIFE
The inevitable bad luck ending up on a fisherman's hook is what's known as...
WORM LIFE
That fateful slumber that got him trapped to a cucumber
He should have cut down on the lazy life and got some exercise...

A TRIBUTE TO WILLIAM THE WORM (CONTINUED...)

WORM LIFE
All the people
So many people
We all stand hand in hand
To remember William and Wormlife...
#wormpop #songsforwilliam

Tesco Staff take a moment to remember at the William The Worm Memorial Bench.

The L D i le

OPEN IN APP

FUNNY   ENTERTAINMENT   NEWS   TECHNOLO   ALL ▾

in Loving Memory of
WILLIAM THE WORM
Killed by a cucumber 2016

⏱ 15 hours ago   ↱ 1.2K Shares

William, The Fallen Tesco Cucumber Worm, Has His Own Golden Plaque

What I learned from this post is the internet loved the kind of unconventional behaviour we'd seen from a big company such as Tesco. So it got me wondering, how could I recreate that?

That's when it hit me: I had to become the company or at least appear to be them. So I set up a profile on Facebook called 'Customer Support'. I'd then change my profile picture to the chosen company's logo and I was all set to hit their Facebook page and answer complaints. Not everyone would fall for my method of course, but I found those who were the most pissed off already would be too angry to notice I wasn't the real deal. I would pick the complaints I answered carefully. Not everyone was a target. Some people had genuine complaints and a right to be upset.

For example, a lot of my followers at one time would urge me to hit the complaints on Thomas Cook's Facebook page following the company going bust. Although there were hundreds of complaints waiting to be answered, these people were at risk of losing holidays they had paid thousands for and ultimately there were staff on the brink of losing their jobs. The last thing I would want to do is make the lives of these people any more stressful. My targets became those who moaned over the petty things in life. Those who think it's ok to scream at someone in customer service because their cup of coffee is a degree cooler than usual, often in a blatant attempt to get something for nothing. Losing our minds over the small things in life, that really don't matter, is what leads to the demise of our own mental health.

And I guess that's the point, really. Not only am I on a mission to make people laugh but I hope I can make some of those serial complainers take a step back and realise just how ridiculous they're being.

Some might argue I'm just a desperate guy seeking approval and attention, and you'd probably be right. But what's also true is that it makes me feel great to bring laughter and order to the world of customer support.

Truth is, right now I feel more amazing than ever...and after reading this book, I hope the laughter makes you feel just as amazing too.

INTRODUCTION

When we hear the word 'troll', many of us probably think of an unsightly mythical creature. For some, the small 90s plastic toy with the bright hair will spring to mind. More recently, the word has taken on a much more sinister meaning. The birth of the internet and enormous growth of social media has enabled all of us to share our views and thoughts with millions of people in just a few clicks. But be warned, our posts are open to attack from internet trolls – someone who purposely disagrees or comments with an unpopular and often outrageous opinion to purposely provoke anger.

And then there's me... an internet troll who's turned the game sideways. Instead of anger, I seek to provoke only laughter while my victims are those who are already seriously miffed. Companies' Facebook pages are my stomping ground, where disgruntled customers are there in their droves.

My method is simple: using my Facebook profile called 'Customer Support' and by changing my profile picture to the relevant company logo, I'm able to fool those customers into thinking I'm the real thing. My aim? To turn those frowns upside down, get people laughing and for folk to take a step back and not take life so seriously.

But of course, with great power comes great responsibility. It's my gift, my curse. Who am I? I'm The Amazing Troll-Man, your friendly neighbourhood troll.

Here are some of the conversations that took place on Facebook with the customers I fooled. Identities have been hidden to protect the gullible.

THE CUSTOMER ISN'T ALWAYS RIGHT

They say "the customer is always right". Well maybe I'll buy that if they are reading this and are ready to admit just how wrong they were.

MR PID

Stu ▮▮▮▮▮▮▮ **> Costa Coffee**

Its bout time you hired some proper barristers if you charging these prices they dont know what there doing. You should change your name to costa-fortune

Customer Support

You need a Barrister to defend you for your crimes against the English language. Unless you meant Barista, in which case maybe you should change your name to Stu-pid.

Stu ▮▮▮▮▮▮▮

Who TF are you talking to like that on your minimum wage. You cant speak to me like that when it's your job.

Customer Support

Yeh yeh, tell it to your Barrister. Now is there anything else (other than grammar) I can help you with today Mr Pid?

THE BIGOT BUTTY

 ▬▬▬▬ **> Marks and Spencer**

A LGBT sandwich is this a late April fools? Will you be doing a straight sandwich or is it special treatment for them as usual? Are you going to be selling a sandwich to celebrate being normal? This country is a absolute joke we favour foreigners and homosexuals over our own. Wake up and look after.

 Customer Support

Don't have a hissy fit Adolf, we have a sandwich for you 'normal folk' too. Introducing the 'Bigot Butty' served on a delicious white bap (none of that foreign brown muck). These perfectly round baps are such beauties they wouldn't look out of place on page 3 of the daily sport... that'll keep the gays away. Topped with lashings of bacon, repelling any Muslims within an 8 mile radius. Best served while not wearing a white sheet over your head. Available now, don't choke on it will you.

▬▬▬▬

Im disgusted that you think you can reply like that proves me point.

 Customer Support

Dry your eyes Donald Trump, you're not the only one here who's disgusted. Before you can prove a point you need to have one and the closest you've got to having a point is being a prick. Is there anything else I can help you with today?

TRIGGERED TO THE MAX

Max Hold > Virgin Media

Where do I address a complaint to?

Customer Support
Your mum for naming you after a tin of hairspray?

Max Hold
It's my stage name not that I have to explain myself to you. Inappropriate. I have screenshot this conversation and I will be sending it with my complaint. Had enough of this now.

Customer Support
Ooh you're wella hard.

AUTO CORRECT

███████ > **Argos**

The staff in your Arndale store are a disgrace. As I waited for my order I watched three of them messing around and giggling. It was like a youth club. Is there a reason that you employ predominantly miners

---

Customer Support

They have to work somewhere now all the pits have closed.

███████

My phone autocorrected that It was meant to say MINORS but I suspect you knew that. Clearly you're one yourself with that childish response.

Customer Support

And clearly you're a miserable count.
Damn you're right about that auto correct.

THE FOLLOW THROUGH

[redacted] > **Tesco**

There was a terrible smell this morning at the entrance to the big Tesco store Chesterfield near the customer service desk and self service checkout. Not very nice when you're shopping for food.

Customer Support

Rumour has it.. Linda who works the self serve checkout gambled on a fart and it didn't fall in her favour, if you know what I mean? We had to lend her some tracksuit bottoms from lost property and everything. Soz.

[redacted]

Ok thanks

KING OF CAPS

[redacted] > **Argos**

FFS BEEN ON HOLD AGES CAN SOMEONE PLEASE HELP ME

Customer Support

Yes sure, the caps lock key is the one above 'shift' and 'ctrl'. Hope this helps.

EMPATHETIC

▮▮▮▮▮▮▮ > **Walmart**

Who the hell is in charge of hiring in Burleston, TX? I saw one female staff member in full rage shouting and crying in front of us all. Other workers seemed to allow this to happen and stood with her casually chatting if this was the norm. Why wasn't she taken into the back away from customers. It's unacceptable to make a scene like this she shouldn't be working there in the first place if she's that unhinged. I'm no shrink but that's one crazy b you got working for you.

Customer Support

Thank you for this. Maybe she'd received some bad news? Or maybe she'd something major going on in her personal life. You could have shown empathy, you could have checked if she was ok? Or you could have minded your own business and got on with your day. But nope, you came here to shame her publicly. I'm no gynaecologist but I'm pretty sure that makes you one nasty c...

Wow someone is getting fired !!

Customer Support

Wow wrong again c▮▮▮t chops.

25

SOMEONE NEEDS A HUG

 ▨▨▨▨▨ **> JD Sports**

Staff are wankers

 Customer Support
Ricky, where's all this anger coming from? Sounds like someone needs a hug x

fuck off pedao

 Customer Support
Pedalo?

▨▨▨▨▨
PEDO

Customer Support
Pedro?

PEEDO

Customer Support
Speedo?

fuckin keyboard warrior cum round mine and see you act up then

SOMEONE NEEDS A HUG (CONTINUED...)

Customer Support

What a splendid idea!! I could give you that hug you desperately need? Maybe we could go for a nice country walk or go for that pedal boat ride that we've always talked about. Send me your address and I'll be round in the morning.

Be sure to have the kettle on!

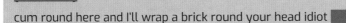

cum round here and I'll wrap a brick round your head idiot

Customer Support

There once was a man called Rick,

Who to be fair was a bit of a prick.

I tried to show him some love,

But all he wanted to do was give me a shove,

And finish me off by hitting me with a brick.

I thaaaaannnkkk yoouuu, Goodnight. 😎

GIFT WRAPPED

 ▓▓▓▓▓▓▓▓ > H&M

I see H&M are the latest to jump on the gay bandwagon. What you doing for straights? I will be boycotting

Customer Support
Such ugly words on such a pretty background, it's like you've gift wrapped a turd.

▓▓▓▓▓▓
Whats the background matter or have to do with you? I have it on all my posts. I'm stating facts not asking for debate. I don't want to see same sex couples all over each other just so you can sell clothes. What you have said just shows you up as rude. Either simply acknowledge my feedback or say nothing at all.

Customer Support

Thank you for your feedback

Vile I don't get how you get away with this. You won't be seeing me in your stores again.

 Customer Support
C'ya, have a gay day. 💕

I COME IN PEAS

_____ > Tesco

A dead slug in the sugar snap peas I bought today which are now ruined. Disgusting! Can someone get back to me about this please!

Customer Support
You have my deepest sympeathy, may he rest in peas 💜

_____

Immature and not helpful at all. I'm not being funny but Slugs carry parasites which can be harmful so I expect you to take this more seriously or I will go to the press with my evidence.

Customer Support
Press? Bitch Peas!

I COME IN PEAS (CONTINUED...)

How rude are you I would expect to lose your job speaking to me like that. It's not funny and if you think I will just walk away you dont know me trust me. Tell me how I can speak to a manager because this is not on.

Customer Support
I've notified my supervisor that we have a customer irritated with her-peas

Youre pathetic I will phone up and find out who you are and who is your manager I'm disgusted!

Customer Support
I'm Peater

You're pathetic.

Customer Support
Yeh I know, peas out ✌

STAND AND DELIVER

 ▮▮▮▮▮▮ **> Amazon.com**

what you have done is theft and I have being lied to its all a big scam I wont be buying off here again I wouldnt expect a company as big as amazon to be liars

---

 Customer Support
What's been stolen? Your full stops?

▮▮▮▮▮▮

Are you serious you are taking the piss now and money is all you care about you didnt deliver my razors and still haven't refunded me even tho I was told you would. Just because its not much money doesnt mean you can just keep it. Its theft at least dick turpin wore a mask

Customer Support
You mean Bic Turpin.

▮▮▮▮▮▮

your not funny and boring me now count yourself lucky am not taking this further got better things to do with my time than you idiots

Customer Support
Phew, close shave for us.

CARTEL PARK

 Susan ▮▮▮▮▮ > Tesco

Still nothing has been done about the large groups of individuals who park up all night in the car park at ▮▮▮▮▮ Tesco in ▮▮▮▮▮. It's getting beyond a joke.

TESCO

Customer Support
Just to be clear, you're complaining about the presence of cars in a car park.

Susan ▮▮▮▮▮
No I'm complaining about loitering youths in cars who are not customers. They are intimidating and potentially dangerous individuals who have no business being there. They always look suspicious and could be peddling drugs for all you know. I also think your response is very rude.

TESCO

Customer Support
Ah sorry, I think what's happened is your phone is auto correcting cartel to cars thus making your complaint seem quite ridiculous.

Susan ▮▮▮▮▮
You have to be joking me? is this anyway to speak to a customer with a legitimate complaint. I had hoped you would have taken this more seriously as these are gangs who for all you know COULD be involved in criminal activities / drugs etc, not to mention breaking COVID rules and you are not bothered. Shame on you.

Customer Support

It's Pablo Tescobar.

Susan ▮▮▮▮▮

Unbelievable you are continuing this. You will be losing my custom now I will simply shop elsewhere it's no bother to me. I'm getting this flagged. Absolutely bizarre behaviour.

Customer Support

Shopping elsewhere doesn't come without it's dangers. You could bump into Aldi Capone.

Customer Support

...and then there's Spar Face of course.

Susan ▮▮▮▮▮

Who do you think you are talking to me like this and why is no one monitoring the output here. As a business owner myself I would be mortified if my staff behaved like you, you'd be gone in an instant! I'd be surprised if you aren't dismissed for this. What is going on?

Customer Support

Am I being head hunted? So what's this job you're offering me?

Susan ▮▮▮▮▮

This is getting too bizarre what on earth are you on? Never would I employ someone like you.

Customer Support

I could do with a new job, hours here are shit and the boss is horrible. He's always saying things like "you don't work here anymore, how did you get in" and "you know we've got a restraining order against you" you know the sort of things bosses say. I can start pretty much straight away. I've no formal training as such but I'm as versatile as a smack head's teaspoon and I'm very punctual give or take a couple of hours.

Just as long as it's not a job in leisure, I'm ban from all uk swimming pools you see. It was a terrible misunderstanding that's all. I forgot my glasses and mistook a gentleman's trunks for my hanky. Anyway the judge wouldn't have it and as it was the 6th time I'd forgot my glasses that week so he issued the ban and put me on tag... oh that's the other thing, I can't do evenings, I need to be home for 6pm sharp.

Susan ▮▮▮▮▮▮

What have I just read. What are you playing at? You are going to cause a lot of trouble for your company. You need to grow up.

Customer Support

Oh Susan, just when I thought we were bonding and the interview was going so well you have to put a downer on it with your negative vibes. So, how many breaks do I get?

Susan ▮▮▮▮▮▮

Who the hell are you to pass comments about me? This whole thing is totally bizarre and I'm flagging it so maybe you should think about what you're doing. I am actually a very positive person but I will not put up with your crap.

CARTEL PARK (CONTINUED...)

Customer Support

Not being funny Susan but I've seen more positivity in a Wish review. I hope you're going to perk up a bit when I'm working for you.

Susan

I've now gone from being shocked to bored. I've had enough so go and waste your time annoying someone else because I'm not interested. I've flagged this so nothing else to say.

Customer Support

Ok see you Monday

Susan

Dream on.

Customer Support

Tuesday it is then, have the kettle on.

SKY'S THE LIMIT

 Diana ▮▮▮▮▮ **> Sky**

No internet for two days and counting. Called up twice and basically told it's my equipment but a quick google search and the complaints on here show that SKY has had an outage for the last two days. When is someone at Sky going to own up that it's their fault and take responsibility. Is honesty too much to ask?

 Customer Support
Yeh what happened is Barbara bet me that I couldn't put one leg up in the air and lick my own arse like a cat. I would have managed it if it weren't for those bloody spinny chairs they have us sit on. It went flying into the server cabinet and well... you know the rest, you've got no internet and I'm down a fiver and a packet of Hobnobs. So yeh, I take responsibility but I'm sure we all agree that Barbara had a hand in this too.

Diana ▮▮▮▮▮
What are you prattling on with? It sounds like your drinking on the job. It's very much out of order!!

 Customer Support
You're damn right Diana. It's as out of order as a Maccy's milkshake machine. She knew it wasn't possible to do it on one of those chairs. I was cheated for sure.

Diana ▮▮▮▮▮
Who manages you I think I will speak with them please?

Customer Support

Yeh that would be Barbara but she's a bit busy at the minute seeing if she can fit 5 hard boiled eggs up her bum. Time to win those Hobnobs back.

Diana ▮▮▮▮▮▮

I've copied this chat and I will be reporting it and sending it in.

Customer Support

Where to, Guinness Book of World Records?

Diana ▮▮▮▮▮▮

No to a newspaper.

Customer Support

Ask them to go with the headline 'double or shits'.

THE AMAZING SPIDER-MOAN

 ███████ > **Tesco**

was spoken to like shit today at the ███████ Tesco for putting one foot on a bottom shelf to reach a product on the top shelf. How am I supposed to get it without climbing up a bit? Why put shelves that high in the first place? The guy who spoke to me was obviously on a power trip because he's wearing a Tesco uniform which is pathetic really. Just because you work there it doesn't mean you get to tell me what to do.

TESCO

Customer Support
And just because you sit on the web all day with a sticky hand, it doesn't mean you're Spider-Man.

███████

Sorry what?

███████

@The Sun

TESCO

Customer Support
@The Daily Bugle

THE ARGOS BIKE

 ▬▬▬▬▬ > **Argos**

FFS WHY DONT YOU HAVE ANY BIKES

 Customer Support
We do, She's called Sandra and works in the warehouse. Been in more beds than Alan Titchmarsh's trowel that one.

▬▬▬
Your reply is beyond any comprehension I'm going to be sharing this with my followers so everyone knows what your like and this is especially inappropriate when I wanted a bike for my sons 13th birthday.

 Customer Support
Yeh that would be inappropriate, maybe we could hook him up for his 21st.

▬▬▬▬
WTF! is this customer policy to speak to customers like crap?

 Customer Support
Of course not. Let me know when you buy something.

You should know that I have a lot of followers on YouTube and I will be sharing this with them you horrible twats

Customer Support
You couldn't get followers if you were the front of a conga.

Actually I have got many thousands thank you and we review purchases and companies so you won't be happy when I tell them not to buy bikes toys from you especially as I have lots of children following me

Customer Support
Oh Pied Piper down will you.

COLD AS ICE

 **> Tesco**

Absolutely appalling behavior of staff at today when i over heard three male staff making comments about having sex with someone on the freezers. I made a complaint on my way out and it was brushed off by the manager who said they were joking and weren't your staff and were a company you'd brought in to do a stock take. Your staff or not they are technically employed by you and under your control. I don't expect to hear it and it's put me off you and frozen veg for life.

TESCO

Customer Support
They meant no harm, they cum in peas.

I don't find that funny at all. will be spending my money with your competitors from now. It beggars belief that both the manager and you do not listen to or care about your customers and think this is funny when it is not.

TESCO

Customer Support
What can I say, we're a bunch of cold fuckers.

TIS THE SEASON TO BE TROLLY

Christmas is a time for love and cheer, a time for family and loved ones, a time for making memories and a time for losing our shit on Facebook over that order which never arrived.

SERVING SUGGESTIONS EXPLAINED

Sharon ▮▮▮▮▮▮ **> Marks and Spencer**

This year as always we purchased the Oakham turkey that serves 6 – 8. There was 4 of us for dinner and we had a few slices cut thinly and there are just a few slices left over. No way would this have served 8 people. Are the 6 – 8 people in your description all on diets? However it was lovely and so were the carrots served with orange segements.

M&S

Customer Support

Hi Sharon, thanks for getting in touch. In the interests of diversity and not to offend any minorities, the serving suggestion of 6-8 people would have included one vegetarian / vegan and two persons belonging to religious groups that don't celebrate Christmas and / or don't eat turkey. Hope this helps.

Sharon ▮▮▮▮▮▮

Do you put this on your packaging as I don't recall seeing this, feels more like april fools day

Sharon ▮▮▮▮▮▮

I think you should send me a voucher as I have just split my side laughing at your crazy response.

Marks and Spencer

Hi Sharon, thanks for flagging this with me. It's a fake account and absolutely nothing to do with M&S. I've reported it to our Marketing team and we'll work with Facebook to have it removed. Apologies for any offence or distress it's caused. Best wishes, Matt.

Sharon

So in plain English – it serves 3-5!! So why not say so??

Sharon

M&S please can you explain how this is a fake account if it was a reply to a post that I sent to you.

Amanda

Because it was posted in an open Facebook page anybody can reply including pseudo accounts (the reply from whom I found hilarious) the fake account doesn't have the blue verified tick by the name

JINGLE BALLS

 ▬▬▬▬ **> Argos**

Think it's absolutely disgusting to open a game 'boom ball game' to play with my son to find it's got 3 missing bits!! Especially the most important part – the balls!! It's blady Christmas and we now have a toy down! Do not expect a BRAND NEW toy to have missing parts!!

 Customer Support
You think that's bad, on a recent trip to Thailand I came across a pair of balls which I was assured wouldn't be there. But I'd paid my money and as they say... when in Rome.

▬▬▬ As amusing as I found that can you actually do anything about the above please?

 Customer Support
Major surgery and plenty of lube

LAST CHRISTMAS

▬▬▬▬ > EE

bought a contract phone from you as a Christmas present iPhone xr and after 1 week had to take back due to lines on screen. Phone was replaced but then had problems with it crashing all the time. Sent back again and was told this time nothing was wrong with phone when there is. Asked to change phone to a Samsung but told I can't do this until my upgrade date which is nearly a year away so I'm having to put up with a faulty phone. If this doesn't get sorted I will be going back with Vodafone. EE are a disgusting company that aren't bothered once they have took your money.

Customer Support

Last Christmas, you signed up to EE but the very next day you had a faulty display

This year, to save you from tears you're going with Vodafone

One bitten and twice shy

you keep your distance

but our upgrade offers still catch your eye

Tell me, baby

what do you want me to do

When it's been a year

only then can I upgrade you

Merry Christmas! We wrapped it up and sent it

with a note saying, "18 month contract", we meant it

Now you know what a fool you've been

But if we give you free data

you know you'd be fooled again

- *George*

LAST CHRISTMAS (CONTINUED...)

I promise you that you will not fool me again. I don't know in what world you are on thinking that would help me. Are you going to help me or just send stupid George Michael songs as this is beyond a joke now

Customer Support
Jitterbug
Jitterbug
Jitterbug
Jitterbug

very childish of you Im not at all laughing and neither will you be when I go back to Vodafone

Customer Support
Wake me up before you go-go back to Vodafone
Wake me up before you go-go
I don't want to miss it when you say goodbye.
- *George*

YOU BETTER NOT CRY, I'M TELLING YOU WHY...

 ▬▬▬▬ Walker **> Tesco**

I am at the end of my tether now with tesco. I got home to discover I had been over charged DOUBLE for the family lasagne bake. If employees were not so busy arranging their night out and smirking at one another then maybe these mistakes would not happen as she has scanned it twice. Now I have been told I have to make another trip to store to sort this out. I better be compensated for my inconvenience or I will not be back. From reading comments on here it seems I am not the only one who is not happy with you. I for one could write a list a mile long I really could.

TESCO

Customer Support

She's making a list, she's checking it twice
Gonna find out who charged her the wrong price
Mrs Walker is coming to store

She sees you when you're smirking
She knows the price of pasta bake
She knows if she's been double charged
So charge her right for goodness sake

▬▬▬▬ Walker

I can not believe my eyes. I will be coming to store you can count on that I would come right away if you were not closed. I certainly do not want to be dealt with by you your attitude stinks.

Customer Support

Oh... Jingle bells my attitude smells

You wish I'd go away

Oh what fun it is to complain

Instead of enjoying Boxing Day

Merry Christmas Ebeneza

THE GOODWILL GESTURE

> Argos

Absolutely disgusted and so angry I order my son a green bmx for Christmas to open it today to put it together ready for tomorrow to find you have sent me a pink bike. We've called customer services and the help line to be told nothing can be done. My 8 year old sons Christmas is now ruined along with him losing that belief in santa as the only thing he has asked for is a green bike.

Customer Support

Karly we are so sorry to hear this. As a good will gesture we would like to offer your son a free Barbie Doll.

NOT JUST ANY S&M, M&S S&M

 ▬▬▬▬ **> Marks and Spencer**

Really disappointed with your gift selection this year. Where are the offers and gifts for under a tenner. Everything is £15+. Yet another company just out for profit this year and only interested in making money during a pandemic. No morals.

M&S **Customer Support**
We're M&S not B&M. It's an easy mistake to make, I'm dyslexic myself and when applying for this job I thought it was an S&M gig. Imagine my embarrassment when I turned up to the interview wearing a gimp mask. Still got the job tho and the irony is listening to you whinging on is much more painful than having my arse whipped whilst my balls are crushed in a vice.

I want a phone number for a manager now!

M&S I want this dealing with now I will not be spoken to like this.

I need a contact number for management or your corporate office now please. This is what happens when give jobs to children instead of grown ups.

Customer Support

Sorry, I'm back. I was just seeing how many Jaffa Cakes I could fit in my mouth. Managed 13, that's an office record... Roy Castle would be proud! Now where were we? Oh yes that's right you were telling us how you're tighter than a smack head's belt. Do continue...

A few moments later the post disappeared but she was soon back with a new post still demanding for a manager to contact her. To my surprise I was still able to comment...

I would the contact details for your corporate office please or someone in management. I would like to report a member of your staff for their disgusting conduct on here which I expect you'll have some BS excuse for like you've been hacked but save it because I'm not buying it.

Customer Support

Word on the street is you won't buy anything over a tenner never mind an excuse.

You do realise I have all the evidence I need on you and I will terrorise your facebook until I get the information I need to report this. You've made a big mistake here.

Customer Support

Terrorise? Who are you, Osama Bin Karen?

NOT JUST ANY S&M, M&S S&M (CONTINUED...)

Carry on hanging yourself it's fine by me as your corporate office will have to send compensation bigtime for this. So carry on all you like.

Customer Support

Be sure to include your address in any correspondence so we know where to send your fuck all filled envelope.

THE PASSWORD RESET

My 'Customer Support' account attracted some attention that I did not expect. I would from time to time receive direct messages from customers believing they were speaking to the relevant customer support department they were seeking. On one such occasion a lady called Rosemary contacted me requesting a password reset for her online casino Facebook app. I can only assume that in her frustration she typed 'Customer Support' in the search bar and up popped my spoof profile. As you can imagine, I was more than happy to help...

THE PASSWORD RESET

I had to factory reset my phone and want to get back into my account. user name: Jerseygirl

Customer Support

Thank you for contacting customer support. We look after many companies. Can you please tell us which account you require a password reset for?

Huge Casino

Customer Support

Ok, I need you to answer the following security question you have set up on your account: Would you rather smell strongly of cheese or faintly of fish?

Fish, I guess, don't remember!

I can tell you I have over 4 billion as of this AM when I played

THE PASSWORD RESET (CONTINUED...)

Customer Support

Unfortunately you had selected 'strongly of cheese' as your answer. Not to worry I can reset your security questions for you as you have extra security set up on your account. Here is the password hint you set up: 'Shit in my neighbour's bin'

Hello?

No, I would never use that password hint

Can you please help me get back into my huge casino account?

Customer Support

Hi Rosemary, as you have mentioned, You have 4 Billion in your account so you have to appreciate security is paramount and we need to go through the relevant security checks. With regards to your above password hint have you ever passed faeces into your neighbours bin or anyone else's bin for that matter. Your password may be related in some way to such an incident.

Never

THE PASSWORD RESET (CONTINUED...)

Customer Support

There is no judgement here Rosemary and we appreciate you may have done this as a joke.

For real, I've never done that

Customer Support

Ok I will see if I can retrieve an earlier password hint on your account. Please bear with me while I retrieve this information.

TY!

Customer Support

Hi Rosemary thank you for waiting. Unfortunately there are no earlier password hints set up on your account. I have spoken with my supervisor and he is happy for me to reset your password by photo verification. Could you send me a photo of an official photo I.D you have. You may cover any personal information such as your address. Your name and photo is all that needs to be visible.

:

Yes I'll take a pic n send it now, TY

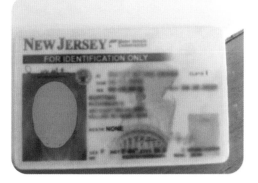

:

Terrible pic! Lol

Customer Support

Hi Rosemary whilst we can now verify your identity your account has you listed as being Nigerian in nationality. We appreciate this is an error but in order for our photo recognition to accept your photo verification we will need another facial photo of you wearing dark makeup or bronzer so you look Nigerian in appearance. We apologise for the inconvenience but this is the only way our systems will accept your photo verification and there is no way of manually overriding this.

:

Seriously?

THE PASSWORD RESET (CONTINUED...)

Customer Support

I'm afraid so. I know it's a lot of trouble but our photo verification is sensitive and can not be overridden manually. The good news is once we have passed verification I can issue you with a password immediately.

Ok, do I have some time here?

Customer Support

Yes take your time, there is no rush.

I can send you the photo I use on my huge casino profile

:

?

:

That should do it

THE PASSWORD RESET (CONTINUED...)

Customer Support
Unfortunately not that photo is not secure and it will need to be compared to your official ID. The colouring of your photo is essential.

Ok let's try as there is not a photo if me dark, my Ancestry DNA says I am 99% Irish!

Customer Support
Could you maybe put a dark stocking on your head. It's worth a try to get passed the auto system. Once cleared I change your nationality too.

Maybe, I'll try...

That looks like I'm robbing a bank!

Customer Support

Let me try processing this now. Please bear with me.

K

Customer Support

Hi Rosemary. Our system will recognise this photo but it's displaying an error saying 'eyes closed'. Could you maybe cut out two pieces of paper drawing eyes on them and sticking them in place so we can resolve this error. Once done I'm confident the system will accept your photo verification.

Ok, lol

I hope you're enjoying this as much as I am, lol

Customer Support

Thank you Rosemary. Just an extra thought before I process this, it may be wise for you to add some lips in the same way. Maybe colour these with lipstick. We only get 3 attempts before the system locks us out for 24 hours and I'd like us to get this right on our next attempt. This way we will have all bases covered and we can get you back in your account. Is that ok?

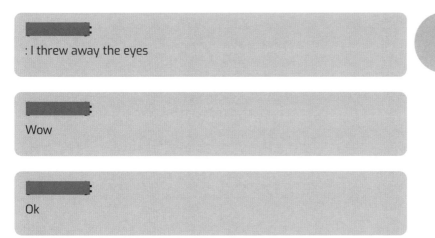

: I threw away the eyes

Wow

Ok

Customer Support

Thank you, sorry for the inconvenience

Customer Support

Hi Rosemary I will process this now

:

OK

:

]: I can't help but to think you are having a bit of fun with me

Customer Support

Congratulations, your photo verification has been successful. Your nationality has been changed from Nigerian to American and your new password is: IshitinBins777 please note passwords are case sensitive. Thank you and have a nice day

SOLVED BY SONG

"I've always thought people would find a lot more pleasure in their routines if they burst into song at significant moments." *John Barrowman.* John, hold my beer.

THE FRESH PRINCE OF CORNED BEEF

 Mike ▣ > **Tesco**

What's happening with the corn beef? A good two centimetres missing from the tin. It's usually full?

Customer Support

Now this is a story all about how,
Mike's life got flipped turned upside down,
And I'd like to take a minute just take a seat,
And I'll tell you all about Mike and his Princes Corned Beef

In Tesco is where he was taught and raised,
On the tinned meat aisle is where he spent most of his days,
Chilling out maxing relaxing all cool,
Shopping for tinned meat the type that's oldskool,
When he picked up a tin that was simply no good,
It contained much less meat than he thought it should,
This one little tin caused him so much despair,
He wrote a complaint to Tesco Customer Care.

I saw his complaint and when I got near,
I thought how do I know he even bought it here,
If I could say anything, where's the receipt,
But I thought nah forget it,
yo refund his corned beef
- *Will*

 that's brilliant

DID SOMEONE SAY QUEEN?

 > Tesco

To whom it may concern. I have just had a terrible experience in the tesco extra in Loughborough. I have got back home to discover I have been over charged for several items that were meant to be on the buy 3 for two offer these being the mini savoury egg bites, cocktail sausages and mini pork pies. I have bought these items multiple times and the offer hasn't shown on any of them. It might be my error but I called the store to ask and was abruptly told that I would have to come to customer services with my receipt. I know I should have checked my receipt before leaving but was a little harassed as I had my two young children in tow while trying to buy food for a kids birthday party tomorrow. Now I have to make another trip to sort and with the amount of effort that will take and endless queuing at this busy time it's hardly worth it. Is there anything you can do to sort this without me having to go back to store. I'm not asking to be treated like the queen but as a single parent some help would be appreciated.

TESCO

Customer Support

Is this the real life?
Is this just fantasy?
Overcharged for a pork pie,
and queuing for an eternity
Open your eyes,
Look at the price of pies and see...

DID SOMEONE SAY QUEEN? (CONTINUED...)

Lol that has made me laugh even tho you haven't answered my question at all your lucky I love queen. I forgot fruit in the rush I was in so I have got to go back anyway now so will sort it there.

Customer Support

I see a little silhouette of a pram,
Scaramouche, Scaramouche, she's back to buy some mango.
Thunderbolt and lightning,
Very, very delighting me.
(Galileo) Galileo.
(Galileo) Galileo,
Galileo Figaro
MAGNIFICO-O-O-O

dying here love it

LOSE YOURSELF

Marcus ▮▮▮▮▮▮▮▮▮▮ **> Aldi UK**

Can you please explain to me why you are limiting the amount of trollies used it makes no sense. I was told I would have to wait for one to return but after queuing for over 20 minutes that wasn't happening and had to try and carry everything in a basket. You provide no hand gel or wipes which there is no excuse for as your staff have them so I had to use the sleeve of my jacket to carry the basket which had to be washed as soon as I got home (MORE WASTED TIME). You have put limits on some products such as loo roll and eggs but allow bulk buying of pasta so there are none left. When I raised this with staff she just blankly at me and stated we have sold out. YES I COULD SEE THAT! An she muttered some unpleasantries about me to a colleague, VERY UNPROFESSIONAL. I had to go and get the rest of my shopping elsewhere which I will continue to do so. The government advise that we are to shop as infrequently as possible which really should be no more than once a week but you made it impossible to get everything in one shop. NOT GOOD ENOUGH!!

Customer Support

Look

If you had

One shop

One opportunity

To seize everything you ever wanted

In one moment

Would you capture it
Or just let it slip?
Yo
His palms are sweaty, not enough trollies, and baskets are heavy
There's germs on his sweater already, sold out spaghetti
Staff are nervous, but on the surface they look calm and ready
Trying not to drop F bombs, but they keep on forgettin'
A complain written down, parts in capitals to make it loud
He opens his mouth, but only selfish words come out
He must be jokin' how, people laid up choking now
The clocks run out, times up, over, blaow!
Snap back to reality...

Allow me to give you a little advice. We are living in times when a job is not a certainty, so I suggest you take things more seriously. I can take a joke but if you think you can get away with insulting me because you've put it in a funny song you are greatly mistaken. I will be reporting you to your superiors. Seriously grow up.

Customer Support

Allow me to give you some advice...
You better lose yourself in the Aldi, the moment
You own it, you better grab that toilet roll
You only get one shop, do not miss your chance to go
This opportunity comes once a week's time...

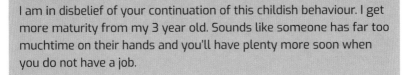

I am in disbelief of your continuation of this childish behaviour. I get more maturity from my 3 year old. Sounds like someone has far too muchtime on their hands and you'll have plenty more soon when you do not have a job.

Customer Support

Sounds like you're caught between being a father and a prima-donna.

MILKSHAKE

 > McDonald's

Can McDonald's please start doing special milkshakes like you do with McFlurry. Burger King's milkshakes are the best, they do Oreo and Kitkat at the moment and they are 👌

Customer Support

Their milk shake brings everyone to the yard, and you're like they're better than yours.
Damn right they're better than ours,
We could make them but we'd have to charge.

😂 😂 😂 😂 I'll pay the extra charge lol

MY TEA'S GONE COLD I'M WONDERING WHY, I GOT...

 ▇▇▇▇▇▇▇ > McDonalds

most ignorant company ever. I've sent several messages now about the poor service we have had at the meadowhall retail restaurant. the manager there isn't interested and it appears that the several messages I've sent on here have been ignored as well. you've ignored me for over a week now. Its your loss as I'll be now taking my business elsewhere. myself, my partner and young brother frequent your store as part of our weekly cinema visit but burger king will be getting our business from now on.

Customer Support

Dear Mc'fan, I meant to write you sooner but I just been busy.

You said your girlfriend's pissed with us too, how is she?

Look. I'm really flattered you like to feed your family our greasy crap,

And here's a voucher for your brother,

It's for a complimentary chicken wrap.

I'm sorry I didn't see your message on here, I must have missed you,

Don't think I did that shit intentionally just to diss you.

And what's this shit you said about you like eat at Burger King too?

Their fries are shit dog, come on, how fucked up is you?

You got some food issues man, I think you need some counselling,

To help your fat ass from bouncing off the walls when you get down some.

And what's this threat about your family boycotting us together?

That type of threat makes me not want to make things better.

I really think you and your girlfriend need each other,

Or maybe you just need to feed her better.

I hope you get to read this letter.

I just hope it reaches you in time,

Before you hurt yourself, I think that you'll be doin' just fine

If you relax a little, I'm glad our food inspires you but man,

Why are you so mad? Try to understand, that we do want you as a fan.

I just don't want you to do some crazy shit,

I seen this one thing couple weeks ago that made me sick.

Some dude was mad and drove his car over to Burger King.

And had his girlfriend in the back and his brother who was just a kid.

And in the front the driver was going crazy ordering fries from the drive through.

Come to think about, his name was, it was you

Damn!

- Marshall

ALL THE PRINGLE LADIES

 _____ > Tesco

Whats happened to the pringles? Theres been none in new street express branch for last two weeks now have you stopped selling them? Same happened with walkers tear and share recently too ? Why do you remove products from shelves from small branches when they are popular? Please bring them back they are my hangover cure 😖 😂

TESCO

Customer Support

All the Pringle ladies, all the Pringle ladies
All the Pringle ladies, all the Pringle ladies
All the Pringle ladies ... Now put your hands up
Up in the pub, fancying some grub and Tesco's is where you've been
You fancied some crisps but now you wanna trip
'Cause your favourites are nowhere to be seen
You looked on aisle 1, you looked aisle two
The staff didn't pay you any attention
Now you're crying tears
'Cause you've had some beers
Ya can't be mad at me
'Cause if you want it then you should've asked in store for it
If you want it then you should've asked in store for it
Don't be mad once you see that we do stock it
If you want it then you should've asked in store for it
Whoa uh oh uh uh oh oh uh oh uh uh oh
Whoa uh oh uh uh oh oh uh oh uh uh oh

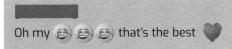
_____

Oh my 😂 😂 😂 that's the best 🖤

AND SHE WOULD WALK 500 MILES

 ▭ > **WHSmith**

hello i would like to know why you are now closing at 5 when it's always been 6.30 before? i walked for over 20 minutes to get there and was very disappointed to find you closed. dont you think you should let customers know about times if they are changing. very annoying as it was a very long walk there and back for nothing

WH Smith

Customer Support

Fuck me, the Proclaimers ain't got nothing on you.

that is not how you speak to a loyal customer you will be in trouble for this I can not believe you have done that

WH Smith

Customer Support

She did walk 500 miles
And she would walk 500 more
Just to be the woman who walked a thousand miles to find a locked store door
Da Da Da Da, Da Da Da Da, Undela Undela Undela la la la.

not funny and you will be in trouble for this I can not believe it

WH Smith

Customer Support

So you keep proclaiming

▣ > **Argos**

Still waiting for my refund from Argos. Really thought I was getting somewhere on Wednesday, but it's all gone quiet again!

 Argos Dave

She got in touch on Monday
We said we'd sort it by Tuesday
She was still moaning by Wednesday, and on Thursday and Friday and Saturday
She chilled on Sunday.
Please allow 7 days for refunds. -*Dave*

Su ▣ > **Argos**

This is a response to my request for Argos to sort out the refund due to me.

How very professional!!! Not funny at all.

Especially as I have been waiting since 25th Nov. and spent over 5 hours explaining and re-explaining to at least 3 customer service people.

A refund was promised at the beginning of December, and I think I was very patient to wait until after Christmas to start 'moaning' again that the refund had not been sorted.

I am now waiting to see if the refund promised on Fri 28th Dec appears in my account.

Be assured Argos Dave that I will be in touch again if it is not! Your message has made me angry now.

Argos Dave
There once was a lady called Su
And moaning is all she would do
She did it so badly
Even tho I said gladly
That her refund I would put through
I thannnkkk youuuu!!!
Happy New Year Su 😃

Kayleigh ▬▬▬▬
Oh petal

Su ▬▬▬▬▬▬
You did not say you would do my refund. On Friday a very polite PM messaged that hehad done it for me, and I am now waiting to see if that goes through.

Argos Dave
SPOILER ALERT it doesn't go through.

▬▬▬▬▬▬ **Brown**
Please tell me you realise 'Argos Dave' is a spoof account and nothing whatsoever to do with the real Argos 😆 😮

Don't tell herthat. She might gain some common sense

Brown fun spoiler

remove this comment INSTANTLY

Argos Dave

There once was a girl called Miss Brown
Who's post made everyone frown
You don't have to approve it
Just shut up and remove it
So I can continue being a clown.
- *Dave*

Su

I have spoken to real Argos reps through facebook and then transferred to Messenger to continue in private, so didn't think it strange when I saw Argos Dave's post to me on facebook. I rarely use facebook except for keeping in touch with family. Dave got me! I admit it. Now I know he isn't a real Argos rep and drunk on the job, his rhymes are quite funny. Yes, I can laugh at myself. Hope you've all had a good laugh too. Happy New Year to all involved here.

Argos Dave

Happy New year Su, I hope I raised a smile

SHANIA TWAIN

[REDACTED] **> TransPennine Express Trains**

Absolutely disgusting that your driver wouldn't let me on the last Leeds to Manchester Twain when it was at the platform and driver was in conversation with the worker on the platform. When I asked the platform worker why he just shrugged. Now I have to try and get a coach home which will take me all night. I will never use you again.

Customer Support

We are weally sowwy you missed your twain.

[REDACTED]

Is this how you think you should treat customers. Obviously Twain was a typo and I can't believe this is the focus of responding to a complaint and you will soon go out of business treating customers like this.

Customer Support

I suppose what you're saying is...

That don't impress you much..

So you missed the train and now you're on a bus

Don't get me wrong, yeah I think you're alright

But its your fault you'll be travelling 'til the middle of the night..

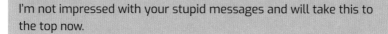

I'm not impressed with your stupid messages and will take this to the top now.

 Customer Support
Oh behave Shania 💕

I WANT YOUR NAME

 ▬▬▬▬▬ **> Sky**

I've just spent 20 minutes on chat with an employee who clearly couldn't be bothered to deal with my complaint and blatantly cut me off. I want the name of this person and chat reference please as I know it's logged this is not acceptable.

 Customer Support
Hi! My name is..
<what>
My name is..
<who?>
My name is.. S-S-S-Slim Shady
Hi there! Do you like whining?,
Shaking your head and rolling your eyes back up into your eyelids?
Wanna report me for everything I did?
Try and get my job messed up worse than my life is?
I arrived half an hour late, I'm tryin to get my head straight

I WANT YOUR NAME

But I can't figure out which one of my colleagues I want to impregnate

And my supervisor said, "Slim Shady you a slacking"

Uh-uhhh! "So what's this complaint? It says you need sacking!"

Well since half twelve, I've felt like a caged elf

who stayed to himself, in one space, chasin his tail

Got ticked off and told a customer to piss off

Got pulled by my boss and I said, "I ain't know customers feelings was gunna be this soft"

My system went down faster than a fat man who sat down too fast

C'mon Shady, sort my complaint dog!

I don't give a damn, Sky sent me to tick the world off!

Hi! My name is..

<what?>

My name is..

<who?>

My name is.. S-S-S-Slim Shady

SCRUBS

▬▬▬▬▬ > Sainsburys

Slow clap Sainsburys for losing a loyal customer for in no uncertain terms calling me liar. I tore my jacket on one of the kids rides at the bottom of the escalator. When I phoned up I was questioned if I was lying and asked A. What I was doing behind the ride and B. why I hadn't reported it at the time. I was retrieving a coin I dropped and I felt my jacket pull but didn't notice it had torn until I got home. What ever happened to the customer is always right. Obviously you think I'm some sort of scrub trying it on to get some compensation well let me tell you I have plenty of money and you won't be getting it anymore.

Sainsbury's

Customer Support
No, we don't want no scrub
A scrub is a customer that can't get no compo from me
Walking round the wrong side of a children's ride
Trying to get something for free...

▬▬▬▬▬
What on earth are you playing at? If you think this is how to deal with complaints I suggest you get more training.

Sainsbury's

Customer Support
I was trained to treat customers with TLC

▬▬▬▬▬
This is ridiculous!

OASIS AT OASIS

[redacted] **> Oasis Fashion**

What's happened to you oasis. I remember a time when you sold decent clothes now it's cheap rubbish no wonder it was in sale should be in trash bin. I returned online order and got an email saying you had received it so why am I still waiting for a refund. Thieving twats give me my money back. No wonder you are going down the pan and having to close shop you won't be missed.

OASIS

Customer Support

Slip inside the eye of your mind
Don't you know you might find
A nicer thing to say
You said that you'd never seen
a company as useless and mean
And hope we fade away

[redacted]

Am I meant to be laughing because this isn't a joke it's theft. I worked in retail for years and would never treat customers like this. I probably know your ceo so maybe I'll take this to them I'm sure it would get sorted then.

Customer Support

So you start a revolution from your bed
'Cause your career in retail has gone to your head.
Step outside, for sale time in bloom
Stand up beside the fireplace
Take that grumpy look from off your face
You ain't ever gonna burn my heart out...

Carry on and see where it gets you makes no sense to joke to an angry customer when you are in the wrong and have stolen money. Sums you up I'll take this to the top now bye

Customer Support

Don't look back in anger.
As you were,
-Liam 😎

ONE BALD MAN FROM FIFE

  > Tesco

the numpty security guard at tesco glenrothes fife gets away with calling me baldy because I dare to question why he searched my wife again! so how am the one thats got band?

TESCO **Customer Support**
Congrats on the band, what's it called, Baldplay?

are yous taking the piss?

TESCO **Customer Support**
Not at all, In fact I'm up for joining this band of yours if you'll have me? I'm not much use as the front man tho, I'm about as outgoing as a nonce in a prison yard. But I did play the recorder at school so as long as you're happy to write all your lyrics to the tune of 'Three Blind Mice' we're golden.

nae having this. how do you think it right to take the piss? is this the way of the world now where companies don't give a flying fuck. How yous nae bothered? what happened to the customer is always right eh

Customer Support
The customer is Right Said Fred maybe.

yous a prick

Customer Support
Come on let's not bicker, we're not the Gallagher brothers, well not yet anyway. What's important now is that we focus on getting this band up and running. Now I hope you don't mind but I've penned us some lyrics based on your struggles, I always think the best songs come from the heart. Like I said, I'm limited to the tune of 'Three Blind Mice but this is a number 1 right here my friend...

One bald man from Fife, one bald man from Fife,
See how he moans, see how he moans,
It all started when shopping with the wife,
Then he ended up getting banned for life,
Did you ever see such a thing in your life,
As one bald man from Fife.

yous on drugs or something. Yous gunna pay for being a dick trust me and jokes on yous because Im nae that bald anyways

Customer Support
Who's your barber, Moses?

ONE BALD MAN FROM FIFE (CONTINUED...)

numpty im gunna take yous to cleaners with this yous bunch of fucking dogshite █ fuck off

Customer Support

Alright mate keep your wig on.

FAIRY TALE ENDINGS

As much as some complaints sounded like a fairy tale, I was unable to deliver the 'happily ever after' they so desperately craved.

WISHES NOT GRANTED

  ▬▬▬▬ **> JD Sports**

not happy the white has started to come off when I rubbed the soul of my max 90s what are you going to do about this

 Customer Support
What were you trying to do, summon a genie?

▬▬▬▬
no I was cleaning them with the shitty wipes you sold me with them fuckin joke I want my money back for lot

 Customer Support
Pipe down Aladdin, you won't be getting any wishes granted taking that tone

JD Sports
Hi ▬▬▬▬
Please ignore the 'Customer Support' account. It is a fake account which we have now blocked and reported to Facebook.
So I can help you further can you please direct message me if your purchase was made online or in store with an order number if you have it.
Thanks

 Customer Support
JD, the block button can be found under the menu titled 'more' on my profile page, let me know if you need any further assistance.

UMPA-LUMPA-DUPADEE-DOO

 > Cadbury World

Omg is all I can really say, wow how this place has changed so very sad. 😔 What ever happened to the factory, seeing how the chocolate was made. Now just a day of queuing for not a lot really. Quit disappointed is all I can say.

Customer Support

We've had to make some changes after it all went Pete Tong. We had one girl have an allergic reaction causing her to turn blue and swell up like a giant blueberry, then some fat kid nearly drown in our chocolate lake. A spoilt brat got attacked by some squirrels and fell into the incinerator and one poor lad got hit by a laser beam shrinking him to half his size. If that wasn't bad enough we had some annoying kid and his grandpa banging on and on about some competition they'd won. The Grandpa was claiming he'd been bed ridden for 20 years but apparently he'd jumped out of bed that day quicker than you can say 'benefit fraud'. To top it off some sick b*stard was enticing kids to steal Gob Stoppers too. So no, we don't let kids see how chocolate is made anymore, more trouble than it's worth.

Good day sir,

Willy

97

COMING TO A CINEMA NEAR YOU

 ████████ > Tesco

The freezers in Tesco in Loughborough were broke again. It keeps happening when it's hot. Why do you not distribute existing stock in the working fridges instead of hiding them away. I spent ages looking for fish fingers in the working freezers but no fish products at all were to be seen. I eventually found a shop worker who then disappeared to find out where the fish fingers were but didn't come back. I then found someone else who disappeared for ten minutes then returned saying he'd found me a box of fish fingers in the back. It was a very frustrating drawing out experience.

TESCO

Customer Support
The new Finding Nemo film sounds shit.

THE LAND OF MAKE BELIEVE

 ████████ > Sainsbury's

You need to staff your customer service desk better especially on days the lottery is on. There was a very long queue and me and some other customers had been waiting about 15 minutes when I walked behind the counter and used the microphone to tell staff we were waiting. Then your embarrassed staff quickly arrived to serve us. On the way out several customers and even some of your own staff came up to me to shake my hand and congratulate me on what I had done. I'm not going to name which store this was as I'm not about getting people in trouble but I think you should speak to all of your managers to make sure staff aren't waiting like this again.

Customer Support
And who would you have play your character in this fictional piece you've written?

I am telling the truth but if you do not want to take me seriously I shall pass my complaint to my influencer friends along with screenshots of this post which will get seen by millions. I do not want to do this and will rethink if you delete your comments. I can only think that it is your last day on the job and someone is feeling bitter.

Customer Support
Oh give it a rest Enid Blyton.

You are unbelievably rude!

Customer Support
It's most definitely unbelievable. Is there anything else, that never happened, I can help you with today?

No

HUMPTY DUMPTY SAT ON A WALL

 ▬▬▬▬ **> Tesco**

Can you please respond to my email dated 18/08/19 with regards to the accident I had on your premises due to an unsafe wall. You know exactly who I am and what this is about. I have spared you the embarrassment of public shaming but that will change if I do not receive a satisfactory response.

TESCO **Customer Support**
Humpty Dumpty is that you?

▬▬▬▬
This is very unprofessional and this total disregard for safety will be held against you I was not going to put a claim against you as hoped this could be settled without the need for court but you clearly do not care about safety and customers.

TESCO **Customer Support**
All the King's horses and all the King's men on way

▬▬▬▬
Why are you trying to provoke me and make me angry. I'm not stupid and won't be lead into this. I will see you in court instead.

TESCO **Customer Support**
I'm not... I feel like I'm walking on eggshells with you now.

FEE-FI-FO-FUM

 ▇▇▇▇▇▇ **> easyJet**

Can you PLEASE answer my messages. I am not happy and need someone to contact me. I was refused an extra leg room seat which I had reserved as it had been sold to someone else I am 6foot 7 and this is the reason I became a plus cardholder so I am guaranteed the extra leg room seats. Been cramped in the small seats ruined the beginning of my holiday because I was in pain for days. I want compensating I have sent lots of emails and messages but I've had nothing back.

easyJet

Customer Support

Hi, please accept our apologies for the delay in getting back to you. Please bear with me while I try to find your original message.

▇▇▇▇▇▇

THANKYOU 🙏

easyJet

Customer Support

Is your message the one that says:
"Fee-Fi-Fo-Fum, I smell compensation"

▇▇▇▇▇▇

no my message does not say that are you taking the piss out of me. This is disgusting and I will be getting compensation for something I have paid for and not got so it won't be funny then.

FEE-FI-FO-FUM (CONTINUED...)

Customer Support
Lighten up Gulliver.

I will not lighten up it is not funny I want my money back for ruining my holiday and injuring me. I want my money back

Customer Support
Would you accept magic beans?

JUST LET IT GO

██████████ > **Cineworld Cinemas**

Visited with my daughter and her friend to watch the premier of frozen 2 and was shocked to see the prices of the food and drink. £3 for a pack of chocolate buttons? It's pure exploitation of parents knowing the kids will pull at heart strings. Refuse to pay that we went back outside to the shop next door to buy the exact same sweets at a reasonable price and sneaked them in. Absolute daylight robbery disgusting.

Customer Support

Let it go

██████████

I will be letting you go by not coming back with that attitude. Unbelievable!

Customer Support

Let it go, let it go
Don't buy our sweets anymore
Let it go, let it go
You got them cheaper from another store
We don't care that our prices you won't pay
You don't have to rage on
Bringing your own sweets never bothered us anyway...

TAKEN

████████████ > E.on

CAN SOMEONE EXPLAIN WHY MONEY WAS TAKEN OUT OF MY ACCOUNT AGAIN AFTER I WAS TOLD IT WOULDN'T BE TAKEN THIS TIME AFTER BEING ON HOLD FOR AN HOUR

Customer Support

I don't know who you are, I don't know what you want.

If you are looking for a refund, I can tell you I don't have money.

But what I do have are a very particular set of skills.

Skills I have acquired over a very long career in customer service, skills that make me a nightmare for complainers like you.

If you drop your complaint now, that'll be the end of it. I will not look for you, I will not pursue you.

But if you don't, I will look for you, I will find you and I will put you on hold.

-Liam

████████████

What that makes no sense?????

IT'S NOT ALWAYS A COMPLAINT

Not everyone takes to Facebook to complain. Sometimes they just want to show their appreciation or make a helpful suggestion. Who am I not to acknowledge these people in my own special way?

WRONG REGISTER

 > People's Postcode Lottery

yess how do I get on the register please

Customer Support
Stealing knickers off washing lines did the trick for me, depends what judge you get on the day tho.

What??

FANTASTIC

 Deb ▮▮▮▮▮▮▮ **> Sky**

So pleased with the service provided for my new router. Even over the xmas time was still delivered on the stated date u said. Customer services polite and very helpfull on the phone. Well done sky

---

 Sky James
Well that's just fanfuckingtastic Deb. Thanks for letting us know and thank you for choosing Sky.
-James

Deb ▮▮▮▮▮▮
been with sky for years wouldn't go no where else 😃

WE'LL PASS IT ON

 > TGI Fridays UK

would just like to say a big thank you to Susie who served us at TGI Fridays Cornerhouse Nottingham last night. She couldn't do enough for us and was excellent with the kids. She deserves a big pat on the back. The Jack Daniels sauce was also as delicious as ever 😄

Customer Support

I'm afraid we had to let Susie go, we caught her shitting in the JD sauce again!! If she shows up to her disciplinary we'll be sure to pass it on.

Thanks for your feedback and we hope to see you again soon.

I don't understand as a company why you'd say that even if it was true? Please tell me this is some sort of wind up?

Customer Support

Unlike Susie, I shit you not.

110

ARE YOU SURE?

  > Sky

I just came off the phone with one of your employees (I'm so sorry I forgot her name!). She is a star and you are so lucky to have her working for your company and I sincerely hope she gets the recognition she deserves. I never really write reviews like this and I am so grateful that I had the chance to speak with her today. She nearly brought me to tears with how kind and understanding she was and she did everything in her power to make things easier for me. She deserves more than a pat on the back for her service today. I would say a Christmas bonus is definitely deserved! She's put a smile on my face this Christmas and I certainly hop you as a company rewards her and give her an awesome Christmas in return! I really can't praise her enough.

Sky James
Are you sure she worked here?

SAVAGELY SETTLED

When I troll my aim is to be playful and ridiculous to lighten up a situation. But there are times when I come across the worst type of people. The aggressive, the bigots and the downright nasty.

COSTA C***

 [redacted] > **Costa Coffee**

I recently ordered a take out Latte at one of your stores only to discover I had the wrong drink after leaving. When I returned I was made to feel this was my fault for picking up the wrong drink when it was handed to me?? I suggest you take names of customers and write on cups like Starbucks to avoid mix ups!!

 Customer Support
There you go..

[redacted]

Absolutely vile sataff I'll be taking this further and I hope you lose your job for this

LORD OF THE WHINGE

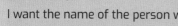 **> H.Samuel**

Bought my wife a ring from h sams in bullring centre. I needed the ring resizing so brought back to be done. Was told it would take 3 days. When I went back to collect they could not find my ring and was told they would contact me when found and would not give me a refund. Absolutely ridiculous I've been waiting over a week with no one giving me any answers. GET MY RING FOUND OR REFUND ME!

 Customer Support
Ok, calm down Frodo.

I want the name of the person who wrote this. You cannot treat customers this way

 Customer Support
The name's Gollum, my precious

OTHER BRANDS ARE AVAILABLE

 _____ > Tesco

So, I have attempted to contact you via messenger but no one bothered to reply.

Who at Tesco is responsible for this?! I am saddened and completely appalled that, in 2019, women STILL have to be subjected to this rubbish.

It's a disgrace and Tesco should be ashamed that they are reinforcing this sort of pathetic and dated gender stereotype.

TESCO

Customer Support

Hey Sweetheart, well spotted! 'Hoover' is of course a brand name and should be replaced with 'vacuum'. 'I'll get our design team to fix this immediately, don't you worry your pretty little head.

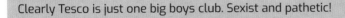

Clearly Tesco is just one big boys club. Sexist and pathetic!

OTHER BRANDS ARE AVAILABLE (CONTINUED...)

Customer Support

Now listen here sugar tits, I resent that remark. All my favourite lap dancers are women. I may be a lot of things, but sexist I ain't!

ANAGRAM

Richard Winchester > McDonald's

had the worst chicken sandwich ever. was completely dry and for some reason the bread had grease on it. had to throw in the bin and was left with just the chips. I got from drive through on the way to work so couldn't return. I expect a refund sort yourselves out this shouldnt happen

Customer Support

Your name is an anagram of 'shit sandwich' what are the chances?

I want the name of the person who wrote this. You cannot treat customers this way

you're an S short so not so smart are you

Customer Support

And you're a sandwich short of a picnic, quite literally.

DO YOU KNOW WHO I AM?

 ▆▆▆▆▆▆ > Tesco

Several DMs sent with no response. Unless you want me to escalate tis with your MD I suggest you respond immediately. Do you know who I am? I suggest you check with your MD.

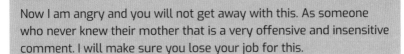

Customer Support

Do I know why you are? I'm afraid I can't help you with that. Have you checked the label in the back of your jumper, mummy might have written it there.

▆▆▆▆▆▆

Now I am angry and you will not get away with this. As someone who never knew their mother that is a very offensive and insensitive comment. I will make sure you lose your job for this.

Tesco

Hi ▆▆▆▆▆▆

The above account is not in anyway affiliated with Tesco. I have responded to your message, please accept our apologies for the delay in getting back to you.

Richard – Customer Care

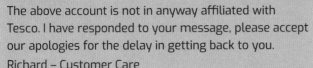

Customer Support

Can I just just say no one wants to admit to being affiliated with ▆▆▆▆ either, including his own mother apparently.

M&S WHINE FOR TWO

 ▬▬▬▬▬▬ **> Marks and Spencer**

I was very disappointed to learn the £12 dine for two offer is no longer available. I bought this every week as a Friday night treat for my husband and I. Tesco will be getting our business from now on and their dine for two is cheaper by £2.

M&S **Customer Support**
Why not treat your husband to a bit of toad in the hole instead?

▬▬▬▬▬
What an irrelevant question. I think you're missing my point. I won't be buying anything from you and I will be buying Tesco's dine for two offer instead.

M&S **Customer Support**
Or maybe you could treat him to a quick ham shank, since it's the weekend?

▬▬▬▬▬
As I've said until the dine for two offer returns I will not be buying anything

M&S **Customer Support**
But whatever you do, don't give him fish fingers.

▬▬▬▬▬
Ridiculous response you obviously aren't listening

RIPPING THE RIPPER

 ▬▬▬▬ > Toolstation UK

WHATS POINT IN HOLDING STOCK AT WAREHOUSE AND NOT IN STORES. NEEDED A ESTWING HAMMER URGENTLY AND COULD NOT FIND A STORE WITH STOCK BUT COULD ORDER ONLINE. HAD TO BUY A CHEAP HAMMER INSTEAD. GET ESTWING HAMMERS IN STORES PLEASE

 Customer Support
Dry your eyes Sutcliffe.

YOU CANT GO OFF LIKE THAT 😆 😆 😆

TIME OF THE MONTH

 > Sainsbury's

I bought a pack of always ultra sanitary pads in store only to discover there were 14 in the pack rather than16 as stated. I do not want to use the rest as the pack has been tampered with. Do I complain to you or always direct. Please advise?

Customer Support

Are you only mad because its that time of the month tho?

Really? How unprofessional to make a rude joke over a personal matter. Absolutely disgusting!

Customer Support

I'm sorry, you're absolutely right. Jokes about a woman's menstrual cycle are not funny. Period!

VICTORIA'S SECRET WEAPON

 ▬▬▬▬ **> Victoria's Secret**

I purchased an underwear set for my girlfriend from metro centre as a gift which was the wrong size. When I tried to return to swap them I was told that you would only exchange the top as the bottoms could have been worn what a ridiculous policy I will not be buying from you again!

 Customer Support

Yeh that store is proper tight. They threw me out of there because I had my walking stick which has an angled mirror on the end of it... and I work for them fam. I'm not going back either, I mean legally I can't go back because of my bail conditions but even so, I wouldn't anyway.

▬▬▬▬

What the hell are you on about you sound like pervert are you for real

 Customer Support

Whoa there Jimmy Savile, I'm not the one buying my gyal peephole bras with crotchless panties and what not so you can get your freak on. Glass houses bro.

▬▬▬▬

I don't quite know what's going on here could you be anymore unprofessional?

Customer Support

I've just sent you gyal a friend request.

Fuck off

A FILTHY MOUTH

Oralene ▇▇▇▇▇▇ **> Argos**

USELESS TWATS!

Customer Support

You've got a filthy mouth for someone who sounds like a mouth wash

Oralene ▇▇▇▇▇▇

FUCK OFF

Customer Support

My pleasure

BAG FOR LIFE

 ▬▬▬▬ **> Tesco**

USELESS! Can you define 'bag for life'?

TESCO

Customer Support
It's what your husband got when he married you.

I have no words you must want to lose your job.

THIS IS SO NOT ON!!

TESCO

Customer Support
And yet it's sounds like you so are.

PRINCE CHARMING

 > eharmony

Waste of money no one ever answers sent 100 messages and not 1 reply and get unmatched all time women are ignorant on here and most past there best anyway you wont get another penny from me bye.

Customer Support

Maybe try being a bit more Prince Charming and less Prince Andrew?

Funny are ya see who's laughing when I put a complaint in about you. It not right when you ripped me off.

Customer Support

Go for it, like the ladies on our site, I too have zero fucks to give you.

125

LET'S GET READY TO BUMBLE

  > Bumble

Looking for a special lady to join me this weekend when I will be in Mayfair on business in nice hotel. You will pay for nothing on the date. I will take you to a very expensive restaurant to get to know you. Must be under 35, slim and not have children. Could lead to relationship. Yes this will be short notice but the date will be amazing for you I promise. Check out my profile and inbox me

Only two days to find you can I pull this off 🙏

Waste of time fake bitches

Customer Support
Hang in there, I'm confident you'll end up pulling yourself off.

I have found someone and didn't need this crappy site to do it I'm cancelling my membership so the joke is on you

Customer Support
That was quick! Whereabouts in your imagination did you meet her?

LET'S GET READY TO BUMBLE (CONTINUED...)

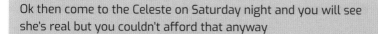

Ok then come to the Celeste on Saturday night and you will see she's real but you couldn't afford that anyway

Customer Support
I hear pretend girlfriends eat free there this weekend.

You are a phoney. I knew something was up so I checked you out and sure enough you don't have a blue tick which you need to show you are a real representative. I think you need to get a life you f**king idiot

Customer Support
Steady on Columbo.

Go away you fake

Customer Support
And yet still more real than your date.

WHAT A NUT CASE

  > Aldi UK

So I receive an email today to my complaint about finding a metal nut in my sandwich telling me that an investigation has taken place and you can confirm that the nut hasnt come from the production line? Well where the bloody hell has it come from? No apology and no refund or compensation for a sandwich i could not eat and could have choked on its not good enough!

Customer Support
Our packaging clearly states 'This product may contain nuts'

Are you joking me or are you stupid this could have ended very badly and imagine if a child had eaten it I want this sorting out SOMEONE COULD HAVE CHOKED TO DEATH

Customer Support
Sounds like someone's got a screw loose that's for sure

This is not on i want a name and reference for this conversation????

Customer Support
No problem,
Ref: Nut Case.

Idiot

Customer Support
Spanner.

BUMBLING IDIOT

 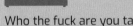 **> Bumble**

What a crock of shit paid membership and it's a total waste of time. The ladies on here don't contact even when you've matched or stop talking to you. Probably fake profiles set up by you to get men to pay for a membership. So much for the happy every after adverts you push.

 Customer Support
With an attitude like that, the only happy ending you'll ever find will be in a Thai massage parlour.

Who the fuck are you talking to you clown obvs a scam when your being like that. You want be saying that to my face I would drop you.

 Customer Support
He said from the safety of a computer screen, in the comfort of his bedroom at his parent's house.

your boring me now got better things to do with my time.

 Customer Support
...like blowing up your girlfriend

COMMUNICATION IS KEY

 ▬▬▬▬▬ **> Virgin Media**

I'm having serious problems communicating with one of your colleagues at the call centre & getting absolutely nowhere. I'm doubtful she's understanding me or my partner & when I asked to speak to a supervisor or senior member of staff, she asked why!

 Customer Support
Hello I Miguel how I help you please?

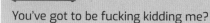
You've got to be fucking kidding me?

WH MIFFED

 ▬▬▬ **> WHSmith**

What a rip off your greetings cards are. A simple anniversary card nearly £4!! No wonder you hide the prices and customers only find out how much they are when it gets scanned at the checkout. I told your cashier to cancel it with all my other purchases. Daylight robbery for a piece of card and bit of paper. You have lost a customer forever.

WH Smith

Customer Support

You should've bought one of our cheaper blank cards and added your own message, something like..

Roses are red,

Your husband thinks our prices are steep.

We dread to think what he's bought you,

because his ass is so cheap.

▬▬▬

I am not cheap I am just not stupid and your not funny message is going to get you in trouble when I put this all in writing to your bosses.

WH Smith

Customer Support

As if you're going to fork out 67p on a stamp

PROFESSIONALISM

  > Sky

How unprofessional, I used the chat function at 11.45. it took until 12.15 to get to a first question, then informed the agent would only be available for another 15 minutes then going offline for 60 minutes, presumably gone for lunch part way through the enquiry.
I can't believe someone goes for lunch while dealing with a customer, I wouldn't be able to do this at my job.

 Sky James
Hi Fiona, don't suppose you know anyone selling an iPhone 6 do you? Cash waiting. No worries if not just thought I'd ask.

Sky James is this a joke

 Sky James
No I dropped my phone and need a new one ASAP. Asking everyone. -James

More unprofessional behaviour

FORGIVE US OUR BINS

 ▬▬▬▬ **> Aldi UK**

Refusing to answer my emails and messages so you've left me no choice but to now make this public. On Friday 16th October I entered Aldi on ▬▬▬▬ in ▬▬▬▬ where I tripped over the badly positioned bins at the entrance. My head missed the product cage (also badly positioned) by millimetres. It's a miracle I didn't hit my head and was killed. No one came to help me and the worker I reported it to wasn't interested with no apology offered! I have sent emails and messages and they have been ignored but what else should I expect from a crappy budget supermarket other than crappy customer service. You have lost my trust and custom!!

 Customer Support
You're like a crappy budget Jesus who nearly died for our bins and rose again to spread this important message. I for one feel truly blessed.

▬▬▬▬

Are you for real?? What the hell was that?? I want an explanation why it's ok for you to make jokes about a serious incident that is endangering lives and I will tell you this if I was Jesus you would be going to hell for this!

 Customer Support
To be fair if you were Jesus I don't think you'd be walking into stationary objects, the man could walk on water.

FORGIVE US OUR BINS (CONTINUED...)

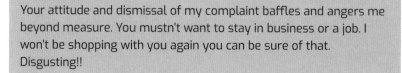

Your attitude and dismissal of my complaint baffles and angers me beyond measure. You mustn't want to stay in business or a job. I won't be shopping with you again you can be sure of that. Disgusting!!

 Customer Support

Don't be like that... forgive us our bins, as we forgive those that trip up against them.

I'll be making a full complaint by letter. This is insane!!

 Customer Support

Put it on Trip Advisor.

A COMPLAINT FROM THE OTHER SIDE

 ▰▰▰▰▰ > Argos

ordered two items for delivery and only one has turned up when I questioned the delivery man he said that it could be because the items are coming from different warehouses but was not sure so I have tried calling for clarification but I cant get through to anyone and my missing item is 146/2355 speaker costing £99.99 so I need to no where it is now please

---

Hello can you answer me please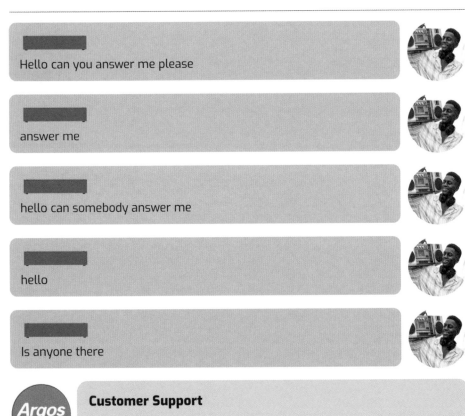

answer me

hello can somebody answer me

hello

Is anyone there

 Customer Support
What's this, a seance?

what a rude way to talk to a customer when I have been left hanging on like this with no response from you despite sending numerous emails and messages so can you just please find my missing speaker please or tell me if another one is coming this is no way to run a company you should look up what the word communication means because this has been terrible

Customer Support

Chill out Derek Acorah. If anyone should be looking stuff up, it should be you on the usage of a full stop. You remind me of a Judge I once had, he dished out unnecessarily long sentences too. 18 months for borrowing from customers packages at my last job. Mad fam!

who on earth do you think you are speaking to I am a paying customer and I will take this to consumer rights now because I am getting nowhere speaking to you I am in disbelief of how rude you are and you obviously should not be doing this job

Customer Support

Come on Derek, what did we say about the full stops?

my name is not Derek so why the hell are you calling me Derek I want to speak with someone high up about this because theres something wrong with you your an idiot

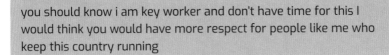
you should know i am key worker and don't have time for this I would think you would have more respect for people like me who keep this country running

Customer Support
I used to work with keys too keeping the Country's noses running, that's how I landed in prison the second time Derek.

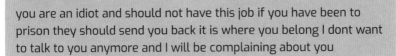
you are an idiot and should not have this job if you have been to prison they should send you back it is where you belong I dont want to talk to you anymore and I will be complaining about you

Customer Support
Nah I ain't going back inside man, you think you're bad with your full stops, the boys in there were brutal when using the colon.

stop wasting my time I will speak to someone else about this you are an idiot

Customer Support
Don't be like that Derek.

Customer Support
Hi Marcus, my name is Havinya. I apologise for my colleague, he's new. How may I help?

does being new excuse him for being rude and an idiot I do not think so and I am not explaining myself again you can read can't you so sort it out

Customer Support

I'm Havinya on Derick, it's me again did you miss me?

I can not believe you think it ok to behave like this in your employment trying to be funny when it is not you are making me very angry you have done nothing to help find my speaker and I will be making a complaint about you

it is me who pays your wages remember that

Customer Support

Wait... you're Tracy from finance?

I am going you are an idiot and I am not dealing with you again I have had enough and will be complaining about you

Customer Support

Ok Tracy, I'm going to pop and see you later anyway. I think my tax code is wrong again.

WHAT THE READERS THINK...

What people are saying about The Amazing Troll-Man...

"Wesley, AKA The Amazing Troll-Man is a bloody legend"
Ozzy Man Reviews

Stacey Rebecca Boyfield recommends The Amazing Troll-Man...
"Amazing page, frequently has me crying with laughter! The amazing troll man is exactly that."

Robert Allam recommends The Amazing Troll-Man...
"This man has a real talent. REAL! Please keep the awesome content coming!"

Kulbir Kaur Eastwood recommends The Amazing Troll-Man...
"Hilariously clever comedy, very well written and super witty!"

Lisa Finch recommends The Amazing Troll-Man...
"Funniest thing on fb. This man owns the internet! 5 trillion stars."

Cally Shanley recommends The Amazing Troll-Man...
"The funniest thing I have EVER seen/read. My favourite comedian. Absolutely hilarious and never fails to make me laugh out loud. Keep it up!!! Please!!!"

Cath Buchan recommends The Amazing Troll-Man...
"Absolutely hilarious and just makes me absolutely pmsl every single time. He's needs prescribed on the NHS."

Pauline Guild Pearce recommends The Amazing Troll-Man...
"Hilarious guy with such a witty & sarcastic sense of humour. Keep them coming 5 stars."

Linda Rose recommends The Amazing Troll-Man...
"If you appreciate British humour, you will love this man. i haven't laughed so much in ages and he is very talented in adapting songs. A genious."

Jan McKenzie recommends The Amazing Troll-Man...

"Fantastic genuine out loud belly laughs – so good for the soul. Thank you Troll-Man."

Helen Elizabeth recommends The Amazing Troll-Man...

"Cried with laughter more than is physically advised for a lady in her fifties. This is the internet at its very best."

Liam Wright recommends The Amazing Troll-Man...

"Quite simply the best page on Facebook, very very clever and absolutely hilarious."

Bridgette Cameron recommends The Amazing Troll-Man...

"Absolutely hilarious! Read in public only if you don't mind embarrassing yourself, giggling like a fool."

Samantha Powers recommends The Amazing Troll-Man...

"Have not laughed so hard in a long time. Brilliant!!"

Nicola Jackson recommends The Amazing Troll-Man

Hysterical never laughed so much. He is the talk of our workplace x

ABOUT THE AUTHOR

Wesley is known on social media for his satirical posts. In 2016 a complaint he made on Tesco's Facebook page went viral. The post known as 'William The Worm' reached people from all around the globe after Wesley and a Tesco employee named Rob engaged in some hilarious banter over the deceased worm. It was this customer-company relationship that gave him the idea of creating a spoof customer service account, and The Amazing Troll-Man was born. Wesley has also used his popular online presence to help two school teachers achieve UK Music Chart Success in 2014. The song called 'Bring It Home' reached number 100 in the Official UK Charts after Wesley released the song under his label 'Band Crusade' and promoted it using only social media.

CREDITS

The Amazing Troll-Man

©2021 Wesley Metcalfe. All rights reserved.

First edition printed in 2021 in the UK. ISBN: 9781910863855

Edited by: Phil Turner

Designed by: Marc Barker, Paul Cocker & Phil Turner

Cover art: Marc Barker

Speedos picture on page 27 courtesy of Alex Proimos
(www.flickr.com/people/34120957@N04)

Published by Unfiltered Books

Unit 1B, 2 Kelham Square

Sheffield S3 8SD

Printed in Great Britain by Bell and Bain Ltd, Glasgow